MW00605302

MINDFUL KIDS *in 10 Minutes a Day*

Four weeks of activities to easily add mindfulness to your school curriculum from preschool to second grade

by Giselle Shardlow

KIDS
YOGA
STORIES

Copyright © 2022 by Giselle Shardlow
Background and accent images/photos courtesy of Freepik.com

ISBN: 978-1-943648-92-4

All rights reserved. No part of this book may be reproduced in any form by any electronic or mechanical means, including photocopying, recording, or information storage and retrieval without written permission from the author. The author, illustrator, and publisher accept no responsibility or liability for any injuries or losses that may result from practicing the yoga poses suggested in this book. Please ensure your own safety and the safety of the children.

Kids Yoga Stories
Boston, MA
www.kidsyogastories.com
www.amazon.com/author/gisselleshardlow
Email us at **info@kidsyogastories.com**.

What do you think? Let us know what you think of *Mindful Kids in 10 Minutes a Day* at **feedback@kidsyogastories.com**.

Welcome to
Mindful Kids in 10 Minutes a Day

• • • • • • • • • • •

This classroom yoga resource is for kids yoga teachers, parents, caregivers, and health practitioners looking for fun, simple ways to add mindfulness to your school curriculum.

To spark your imagination, there are specific sensory activities for each day of the week, with the following themes:

MONDAYS Sound

TUESDAYS Smell

WEDNESDAYS Touch

THURSDAYS Sight

FRIDAYS Breath

The mindfulness practices in this resource should take around five to ten minutes. Use the ideas as a springboard and feel free to add other age-appropriate theme-related yoga poses, songs, breathing techniques, relaxation stories, meditations, art projects, and field trips.

© Kids Yoga Stories

To make your classroom yoga experience as successful as possible, try these ideas:

Create a ritual before each mindfulness session (for example, sit in a circle, rub your hands together, and take a silent moment).

Set up the environment beforehand so the children know what to expect during mindfulness exercises. Slow down, capture their attention, and help them focus.

Create a safe space to try something new and different. Give positive feedback to children who give it a try.

Practice the activities with large groups, small groups, pairs, or individuals—whatever suits you.

Focus on having fun with the mindfulness activity, not on getting it perfect the first time.

Don't worry if your children don't respond to the activity the first time. Think of this as a lifelong practice that evolves over time. Follow their lead and enjoy the process.

Engage the children. Follow their passions and interests.

Create authentic, meaningful experiences. Keep it light-hearted and fun.

Cater to their energy levels and different learning styles.

Be creative and enjoy yourself—the kids will notice your enthusiasm.

Encourage children to make up their own mindfulness activities. Brainstorm other mindfulness activities that fit the various sensory topics.

Encourage the children to share their mindfulness experiences with their families and friends. Or add a note in the parent communication about which activities you're practicing in class.

Discuss the benefits of mindfulness to their health and well-being. Maybe talk about famous people who practice mindfulness and why they do it.

End each week by reflecting on their favorite mindfulness activities, meditations, and games.

Embrace the main idea that is to take a moment to pause and come to the present moment. Feel the benefits of slowing down and calming your mind.

Get children learning, being present, and having fun in the classroom in less than ten minutes a day with these fun and easy mindfulness activities!

Kids Yoga Stories
www.kidsyogastories.com

© Kids Yoga Stories

About
Mindfulness

What is "mindfulness"?

Mindfulness has become quite the catchphrase these days, as educators and families are looking for ways to help themselves and their children release their upset about things that have happened in the past and anxieties about the future. Being mindful is about looking for peace by focusing on the present.

By being mindful, we can learn to live in the present moment, with curiosity rather than judgment. The grandfather of mindfulness, Jon Kabat-Zinn, defines mindfulness as "paying attention in a particular way, in the present moment, and non-judgmentally."[1]

We can focus on being mindful while using our senses, so children can practice just seeing, smelling, or hearing. By practicing paying attention to one thing at a time, they can feel safer and in control of themselves and their environment.

How do we teach mindfulness to children?

The most important step to teaching mindfulness is to begin this lifelong practice of mindfulness for yourself first. Then your own enthusiasm and understanding of the practice will shine through in your teachings.

Mindfulness encourages us to:

1 Notice how much our thoughts are racing and when we're not living in the present moment. Take note throughout the day if you are or aren't present in the moment.

2 Get curious about mindfulness by using your breath to bring you to the present moment. Choose a task that you do every day, and do it mindfully.

3 Commit to a mindfulness practice that works best for you, whether it's at a set time or throughout the day.

Once you're familiar with the mindfulness practice yourself, be confident in bringing the joy and wonder to children. You'll be planting seeds of self-regulation, attention skills, and happiness for life!

---

1. Kabat-Zinn, Jon. *Wherever You Go, There You Are: Mindfulness Meditation for Everyday Life*. New York: Hyperion, 1994.

Where to Start

1 Review the Weekly Schedule on the following pages.

2 Review each week's packet to familiarize yourself with activities and the resources, which include:

- A list of the daily activities
- Printables of the daily activities

3 Extend any activity that the children are particularly interested in or do it again on another day.

4 Celebrate the miracles along the way. Allow space to talk about what they like about the mindfulness activities and reflect on what's working and how you could improve the experiences. Honor the process, not the end result.

5 If you miss a day, don't worry. Just pick up where you left off, then use the activities you missed later in the day or double up on some days. The schedule is meant to be flexible to suit your needs.

© Kids Yoga Stories

Mindful Kids in 10 Minutes a Day

Preschool to 2nd Grade
Weekly Schedule

WEEK ONE

Listening Monday	Smelly Tuesday	Touching Wednesday	Looking Thursday	Breathing Friday
The Sound Count	Mystery Smells	Body Massage	I Spy with My Little Eye	Bee Breath

WEEK TWO

Listening Monday	Smelly Tuesday	Touching Wednesday	Looking Thursday	Breathing Friday
Weather Reporter	The Smelly Feels	My Hands	The Cloud Show	Candle Breath

WEEK THREE

Listening Monday	Smelly Tuesday	Touching Wednesday	Looking Thursday	Breathing Friday
Stop & Listen… What Do You Hear?	The Great Outdoors	Mystery Box	The Rainbow Game	Take 5 Breath

WEEK FOUR

Listening Monday	Smelly Tuesday	Touching Wednesday	Looking Thursday	Breathing Friday
Chime Time	Smell Scavenger Hunt	The Body Tap	Watch It Drop	Pompom Breath

Week One

LISTENING MONDAY
The Sound Count
Close your eyes and count the sounds you hear far away, nearby, and inside yourself. Notice how much more aware and present you are after doing the activity.

SMELLY TUESDAY
Mystery Smells
Present a variety of hidden smelly items (pleasant and unpleasant) and see if children can guess what they are. Use this activity to activate their senses and heighten their awareness of the smells around them.

TOUCHING WEDNESDAY
Body Massage
Moving from your head to your feet, take time to massage your body gently and slowly. Do what feels good to both awaken and calm your body.

LOOKING THURSDAY
I Spy with My Little Eye
Play I Spy to help everybody focus together. You could pick items by color, size, shapes, texture, or distance from you. Practice giving helpful hints and asking thoughtful questions.

BREATHING FRIDAY
Bee Breath
Practice this humming breath to encourage children to be aware of the sound of their breath inside their head. Cupping both ears at the same time helps to intensify the sound, helping them to focus.

© Kids Yoga Stories

The Sound Count

Come to a comfortable seated or standing position. Close your eyes, if that's comfortable. Hold up one hand with your hand in a fist. With each different sound that you hear (for example, a car beeping outside, the fish tank inside the room, or your belly growling), raise one finger to count that sound. After a few moments, ask the children to open their eyes and take turns talking about the sounds they heard. This exercise helps to build their focus and increase their awareness of their environment. As a variation, you could do the activity for a longer time and have them count using their second hand, as well.

kidsyogastories.com
© Kids Yoga Stories

Mystery Smells

• • • •

Bring in a few wrapped mystery bottles containing different smelling items (for example, it could be something natural like a citrus fruit, a fragrant flower, or aromatic herbs). Ask the children to take turns smelling the bottles to see if they can guess what's inside. You could ask questions like: What does that smell remind you of? How does it make you feel? Do you like it or not? If you don't have time to wrap bottles, be creative and put a few items in boxes instead, or blindfold the children and bring out the items one at a time.

Body Massage

Start by coming to a comfortable seated position. Take a few moments to settle into the space and take a few deep breaths. Begin by giving your head a little massage, then move down to your earlobes. Be gentle, and not rough, with your touch. Do what feels good. Move down to your shoulders, followed by your arms and your hands, continuing to gently massage your body. Rub your chest, then your belly, in circles. Lastly, massage your legs and your feet. When you're done, take a moment in a seated position to notice how different you feel after your body massage.

kidsyogastories.com
© Kids Yoga Stories

I Spy with My Little Eye

Play I Spy to help everybody focus together. The leader picks something they "spy," and the other players take turns guessing what it is. The chosen items could be picked by color, size, shapes, texture, or distance from you. Practice giving helpful hints and asking thoughtful questions. This exercise is a great way for children to come into the space and into the present moment.

Bee Breath

As you exhale, keep your mouth closed and make a long "mmm" sound, pretending to buzz like a bee around the garden. Then inhale through your nose, keeping your mouth closed. Repeat the bee humming sound as you exhale. Close your eyes and continue in this way for a few minutes or as long as it feels comfortable. You could also cup your hands over your ears to intensify the "mmm" sound. As a variation, you could imagine making the sound of a train whistle.

kidsyogastories.com
© Kids Yoga Stories

Week Two

LISTENING MONDAY

Weather Reporter

Use your senses to be weather reporters. Go outside (or look through a window), close your eyes, and listen for the different kinds of weather where you are.

SMELLY TUESDAY

The Smelly Feels

Make a list of smells that fit under the two categories of "Happy" and "Mad." Notice how smells can trigger your feelings in unexpected ways.

TOUCHING WEDNESDAY

My Hands

Explore your hands with a number of activities that include massaging your palms, tracing your hand, and creating a pattern inside the handprint. Get curious about your hands.

LOOKING THURSDAY

The Cloud Show

Watch clouds in the sky. Observe the clouds as they pass by and notice the various shapes. Talk about how your feelings drift by just like clouds do in the sky.

BREATHING FRIDAY

Candle Breath

Bring your pointer finger in front of your mouth and blow on it, pretending that it's a candle, flower, or pinwheel. This breathing exercise helps children focus on their breath in a light-hearted way.

Weather Reporter

● ● ● ●

Ask the children to use their senses to report the weather. What sounds do they hear? Is it raining? Is it windy? Or maybe it's snowing? Do they hear the chirps of birds or other animals outside? Ideally, it would be great to go outside to experience the weather. However, if that's not possible, they could view the outdoors through a window.

Build their vocabulary by helping them to describe the different kinds of weather in their area. You might even try repeating this activity throughout the day to see if the weather changes. They could discuss what they hear or paint a picture of the weather they can hear, see, and smell.

The Smelly Feels

Talk about how we can associate different feelings to various smells. For example, the smell of cookies might remind you of your grandmother baking cookies at her house. Or the smell of diapers might remind you of your annoying younger brother.

On a paper, draw two columns: one for "Calm and Happy" and another for "Mad and Frustrated" (or choose other feelings you would like to target). Make a list of smells under each column that you associate with the column heading. Notice how smells can trigger your feelings in unexpected ways, sometimes causing you to have big emotions without realizing where they're coming from. Acknowledging these feelings and understanding the source can help you come back to the present moment.

My Hands

Let's get curious about our hands. First, look at them for a few moments, noticing what they look like. Now, stretch your fingers out wide and then make your hands into fists. Tense your hands really tightly and then relax them. Try this a few times, tensing and relaxing. How do your hands feel now?

Now give your hands a massage, one at a time, rubbing your palms in a circle. Then gently pinch and pull your fingers. Lastly, trace your hand on a paper and outline it in a black marker. With a pencil, spend a few minutes creating intricate patterns inside your handprint. You could show the students sample mandala or zentangle designs for inspiration. Finish up by coloring in the patterns with colored pencils or crayons. Try adding gentle background music during the coloring time.

The Cloud Show

• • • ●

Watch clouds in the sky. Either lie on your back outdoors or pick a spot indoors where you can gaze at the clouds. Observe the clouds as they pass by and notice the various shapes. Talk about how your feelings drift by just like clouds do in the sky. Discuss how emotions are a part of being human and that we all have them. Sometimes big emotions can take over our minds, and we need to find ways to let them drift by so we can make good choices and keep ourselves healthy.

Candle Breath

Pretending it's a candle, bring your pointer finger in front of your mouth. Take a deep breath in through your nose then pretend to blow out your candle. Close your eyes, if that's comfortable. Repeat a few times. The idea here is to take extended exhales to calm the nervous system. You could also imagine that you're blowing a flower or pinwheel.

kidsyogastories.com
© Kids Yoga Stories

Week Three

LISTENING MONDAY

Stop and Listen ... What Do You Hear?

Stop for a moment, close your eyes, and listen for the sounds around you. Listen for two faraway sounds, two nearby sounds, then two sounds right beside or inside you.

SMELLY TUESDAY

The Great Outdoors

Go outside in nature to awaken your senses. What do you smell? What things have the strongest smell in nature? What doesn't give off a lot of smell at all?

TOUCHING WEDNESDAY

Mystery Box

Present a variety of hidden items and see if the children can guess what they are. Use this activity to activate their senses and heighten their awareness of objects around them.

LOOKING THURSDAY

The Rainbow Game

Look around the space for colored items in the order of the rainbow: red, orange, yellow, green, blue, indigo, and violet. This activity helps children to sharpen their focus.

BREATHING FRIDAY

Take 5 Breath

When you need to calm yourself, take a moment to inhale and exhale while tracing your pointer finger around the fingers of the other hand.

Stop and Listen . . . What Do You Hear?

Stop for a moment, come to a comfortable seated position, and close your eyes. Take a few deep breaths and come to the present moment. Then begin to listen for the sounds around you. Listen for faraway sounds for a few moments and then shift to listening for nearby sounds. Lastly, pay attention for sounds right beside or inside you. Once you're done, open your eyes. Talk as a group about what sounds you heard. Were any sounds that you heard different from the others? Which sounds were similar?

kidsyogastories.com
© Kids Yoga Stories

The Great Outdoors

• • • ●

Go outside in nature to awaken your senses. Close your eyes, if that's comfortable, and notice what you smell. Open your eyes and see if you can locate what gave off the different smells. If your learning environment isn't near nature, then bring nature items into the classroom to smell. Transform your space into nature indoors. Notice if the different seasons bring about different smells in nature.

Mystery Box

Bring in a wrapped mystery box containing different textured items (for example, it could include something rough, smooth, soft, or pointy). Ask the children to take turns putting their hands inside the box to see if they can guess what's inside. You could ask questions like: What does it feel like? What does it remind you of? Do you see something else in the room that might have a similar texture?

If you don't have time to wrap a box, be creative. For example, put a few items in basket with a blanket over the top or blindfold the children and bring out the items one at a time. Have the children pay attention to how objects feel and bring them to the present moment.

The Rainbow Game

• • • •

Play the Rainbow Game by looking around the room as a group for something red. Once someone has located something red, then move on to finding something orange. Continue to play until you find things that are yellow, green, blue, indigo, and violet. The key is to find the items in the rainbow order, and make sure that everyone gets a chance to participate. Use the game to sharpen their focus and spark their attention in a fun, cooperative way.

Take 5 Breath

Take your right hand and spread your fingers like a star. Place your left pointer finger at the base of your right pinky finger. As you take a deep inhale, slide your pointer finger up your pinky finger. Pause briefly at the top of the finger. Then exhale fully while tracing the inside of your pinky finger. Repeat the inhale up your ring finger and exhale down your ring finger. Continue tracing your fingers and matching to your breath until you come to the outside of your thumb after five deep inhales and exhales. You can also trace your left hand if that's more comfortable. You could imagine that your pointer finger is going up and down a rollercoaster ride at a fun park.

kidsyogastories.com
© Kids Yoga Stories

Week Four

LISTENING MONDAY

Chime Time

Gently strike a chime and listen to the sound. Close your eyes if that's comfortable. When the sound disappears, put your hand on your chest.

SMELLY TUESDAY

Smell Scavenger Hunt

Go for a scavenger hunt for various smells around your environment. Look for both familiar and unfamiliar smells, and even notice how many things don't have a smell at all.

TOUCHING WEDNESDAY

The Body Tap

Gently tap the various parts of your body, starting with your arms, then your chest, and ending with your thighs. Think about think about waking up your body and boosting your energy.

LOOKING THURSDAY

Watch It Drop

Take time to watch a mind jar, bubbler, or snow globe. Imagine that the floating sparkles are all the thoughts in your mind, both positive and negative.

BREATHING FRIDAY

Pompom Breath

Get out some straws to practice blowing pompoms around the table. This activity is a great way for young children to start extending their exhales to encourage self-regulation.

Chime Time

Come to a comfortable seated or standing position. Ask the children to stop and listen for this activity. Gently strike a chime and listen to the sound. Close your eyes if that's comfortable. When the sound disappears, put your hand on your chest (or anywhere else you decide—on your head, for example). You could then pick one of the children to be the next chimer, and they can lead the activity.

kidsyogastories.com
© Kids Yoga Stories

Smell Scavenger Hunt

Go for an adventure looking for different smells. It could be indoors or outdoors. Either write down all the things you smell, draw pictures, or discuss as a group. Which smells did you expect to smell? Which were familiar? And which smells were a surprise? Spend time activating your senses and getting curious about the smells around you.

kidsyogastories.com
© Kids Yoga Stories

The Body Tap

Start by coming to a comfortable seated or standing position. Take a few breaths to come to the present moment and let your worries melt away. Rub your palms together to gather some heat. Then take your right hand and gently tap your arm going from your shoulder to your hand. Then switch to cupping your left hand along the length of your right arm. Next, tap both hands on your chest while taking a few deep breaths. Lastly, gently tap your thighs with both hands at the same time. As you go through this body-tapping exercise, think about waking up your body and boosting your energy. When you're done, take a few moments to see how you feel afterward.

Watch It Drop

Take time to watch a mind jar, bubbler, or snow globe. Imagine that the floating sparkles are all the thoughts in your mind, both positive and negative. When they settle to the bottom, think of settling your own mind to stillness and calm. Have the children talk about their busy thoughts and the benefits of calming their minds to make good choices and let their worries wash away.

kidsyogastories.com
© Kids Yoga Stories

Pompom Breath

• • • •

Place several cotton balls or pompoms on a table. Use a straw to blow the pompoms around the table. Talk to the children about the effects of a gentle breath versus a hard breath. If you don't have straws, they could blow down their pointer finger, pretending their finger is like a straw. They could also make a net with their two hands and blow the cotton balls within that space, if you'd like the cotton balls more contained and not being blown around the table. You could imagine playing a soccer game and blow the pompoms between goal posts.

kidsyogastories.com
© Kids Yoga Stories

About
the Author

Giselle Shardlow draws from her experiences as a teacher, traveler, mother, and yogi to write her yoga stories for kids. The purpose of her yoga resources is to foster happy, healthy, and globally educated children. She lives in Boston with her husband and daughter.

About
Kids Yoga Stories

We hope you enjoyed your Kids Yoga Stories experience. Visit www.kidsyogastories.com to:

Receive updates. For yoga tips, printables, and kids yoga resources, sign up for our free Kids Yoga Stories Newsletter.

Connect with us. Please share with us about your yoga experiences. Send pictures of yourself practicing the poses. Describe your yoga journey on our social media pages (Facebook, Pinterest, and Instagram).

Check out free stuff. Read our articles on books, yoga, parenting, and travel. Check out our free kids yoga resources and coloring pages.

Read or write a review. Read what others have to say about our yoga books and kids yoga resources. Post your own review on Amazon or on our website. We would love to hear how you enjoyed these mindfulness activities.

Thank you for your support in spreading our message of integrating learning, movement, and fun.

Giselle
Kids Yoga Stories
www.kidsyogastories.com
www.facebook.com/kidsyogastories
www.pinterest.com/kidsyogastories
www.amazon.com/author/giselleshardlow
www.instagram.com/kidsyogastories

© Kids Yoga Stories

YOGA RESOURCES
by Giselle Shardlow

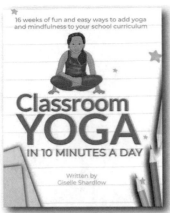

Classroom Yoga in 10 Minutes a Day

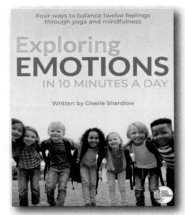

Exploring Emotions in 10 Minutes a Day

Simple Yoga Sequences for Kids

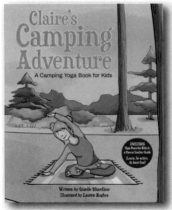

Claire's Camping Adventure

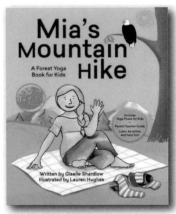

Mia's Mountain Hike

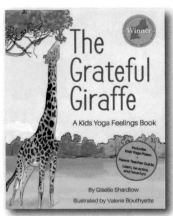

The Grateful Giraffe

Breathing Exercise Cards for Kids

Yoga Poses for Kids Cards
(Deck One)

40 Partner Yoga Poses for Kids

Buy now at www.KidsYogaStories.com/store

Made in the USA
Columbia, SC
25 August 2022

66056520R00022